Penguin Functional English

Pair Work One

Student B

D0525109

Peter Watcyn-Jones

Penguin Books

Penguin Books Ltd, Harmondsworth, Middlesex, England
Penguin Books, 40 West 23rd Street, New York, New York 10010, U.S.A.
Penguin Books Australia Ltd, Ringwood, Victoria, Australia
Penguin Books Canada Ltd, 2801 John Street, Markham, Ontario, Canada L3R 1B4
Penguin Books (N.Z.) Ltd, 182–190 Wairau Road, Auckland 10, New Zealand

First published 1984

Typeset, printed and bound in Great Britain by
Hazell Watson & Viney Limited,
Member of the BPCC Group
Aylesbury, Bucks
Set in Bembo

Contents

To the teacher   *page 4*

1 Getting to know you (1)   *page 7*
2 Getting to know you (2)   *page 9*
3 Missing information: the Eurovision Song Contest   *page 10*
4 Questionnaire: likes and dislikes   *page 12*
5 Who's who?   *page 13*
6 One-sided dialogue: making suggestions   *page 14*
7 Following instructions (1)   *page 16*
8 Missing information: flats and houses   *page 18*
9 Following instructions (2)   *page 19*
10 This is my boyfriend/girlfriend   *page 20*
11 Newspaper interview (1)   *page 21*
12 This is my brother   *page 22*
13 Questionnaire: habits and daily routines   *page 24*
14 For sale   *page 26*
15 Eye-witness   *page 27*
16 Complete the crossword   *page 28*
17 Carry on talking   *page 30*
18 A family tree   *page 31*
19 Going on a weekend course   *page 32*
20 Complete the drawing (1)   *page 34*
21 Complete the drawing (2)   *page 36*
22 Missing information: the life of Elvis Presley   *page 38*
23 Looking at holiday photographs (1)   *page 40*
24 Newspaper interview (2)   *page 41*
25 Looking at holiday photographs (2)   *page 42*
26 One-sided dialogue: shopping   *page 44*
27 Where's the station?   *page 46*
28 Questionnaire: opinions   *page 48*
29 Asking for information about a tour   *page 50*
30 Asking for information about summer jobs   *page 51*
31 One-sided dialogue: an invitation   *page 52*

Appendix: Guide to the structures and functions used   *page 54*

Picture credits *page 64*

To the teacher

Pair Work One forms part of the Penguin Functional English course and was written to give students, working in pairs, further practice in the structures and functions introduced in *First Impact*. The book can, however, be used equally successfully with any other existing functionally-based course at pre-intermediate level.

Description of the material

Like its predecessor, *Pair Work*, *Pair Work One* consists of two books, one for Student A and the other for Student B. [*Pair Work* is similar to *Pair Work One* but is intended for more advanced students (intermediate level and upwards). Included in the introduction to the teacher in that book is the rationale behind using two books instead of one.]

Each book contains thirty-one activities. These are arranged, where possible, into pairs of activities, so that if Student A has one particular role or task in the first activity, then he or she has Student B's role or task in the second, and vice versa. This gives both students practice in the same structure or function, but avoids the possibly boring alternative of simply changing parts and doing exactly the same activity again. Instead of this, the same structure or function is practised again, but the situation (or role) is changed. However, if the teacher and the group would like to repeat activities then there is no reason, of course, why students shouldn't change books and do them again. But this is probably best done at a later date.

The activities can be divided into four main types:

1 Simulations/role-plays
The main difference between a simulation and a role-play is that, in the former, students play themselves but are given a definite task to do or are put in a specific situation and asked to make appropriate responses, whereas in the latter, students are given definite roles to play and are usually asked to assume a different name, background, and so on. An example of a simulation is Activity 14 – For sale, while an example of a role-play is Activity 11 – Newspaper interview (1).

2 One-sided dialogues
These are activities in which students read a dialogue together but can see only their own part, which usually includes opportunities for the student to make his or her own responses. An example of a one-sided dialogue is Activity 26 – Shopping.

3 Information-transfer activities
These are activities in which students are asked to perform a task together; they fall into two types. In the first, one student has access to all the information and tries to impart it to his or her partner. An example of this type is Activity 20 – Complete the drawing (1).

In the second, both students are given access to half the information and, by working together, try to solve the whole. An example of this type is Activity 22 – The life of Elvis Presley.

4 Questionnaires or discussion/conversation activities
These are activities designed to stimulate students to discuss a subject or subjects

with their partner, and usually take the form of a questionnaire. These activities are particularly useful when students are practising giving opinions and showing agreement or disagreement. An example of this type of activity is Activity 4 – Questionnaire: likes and dislikes.

How to use the books

The activities in *Pair Work One* have been written to give extra practice in certain structures and functions. Consequently, they should be done as follow-up work rather than for 'teaching' purposes, since the books assume that the student has a basic knowledge of structures plus the language needed to perform the various functions.

In the Appendix (pages 54–64), a list of the structures and functions for each activity is given, plus examples of typical questions, sentences or responses. Using this as a guide, all the teacher has to do is to decide which structure or function needs practising and choose an appropriate activity from the ones given. Since, in many instances, more than one activity has been written to practise a particular structure or function, repeated practice can be given without the students becoming bored.

Finally, since the level throughout the books is pre-intermediate, there is no need to take the activities in order if the needs of the class and the teacher dictate otherwise. Indeed, it is not envisaged that the books should be worked through from beginning to end: the activities can, and should, be taken in any order depending on the needs of a particular class.

Teaching hints

1 Classroom organization
Since the activities in *Pair Work One* involve the students working in pairs, a certain amount of classroom reorganization may be necessary. If it is at all possible, the room should be arranged in such a way that pairs face one another across a desk or a table. This is to give them 'eye-contact' which makes communication a lot easier. Again, if possible, some sort of screen (e.g. a bag) should be placed between them so that they cannot see one another's books.

However, there may be practical reasons why such a classroom arrangement may not be possible, in which case the teacher can adapt the working methods accordingly to suit his or her particular circumstances.

2 Working in pairs
Since the students will be working in pairs, there is the inevitable problem of what happens when there is an odd number of students in the class. Here are one or two possible solutions (although they are by no means the only ones):

a. The teacher forms the 'extra' partner, in which case he or she should choose a different student to work with each time.

b. The 'odd' student monitors another pair. The student chosen to monitor another pair should be changed each time an activity is done.

c. Three students work together instead of two. Two of the students form a team to partner the third one, taking it in turns to talk to him or her. Again, the group of three should be changed frequently.

One final consideration regarding pair work is that partners should be changed frequently to ensure that everyone really gets an opportunity to work with and to get to know as many different members of the class as possible.

3 Introducing an activity

Clear instructions are given for all the activities, so in most cases it should be sufficient for the teacher simply to ask the students to turn to a particular activity and to let them read through the instructions. While they do this, the teacher goes around the class checking that they have fully understood what they have to do before they begin.

If, on the other hand, the class lacks confidence or is not used to communicative work, the teacher could, on the first few occasions when the book is used, demonstrate briefly with two students (A and B) while the class monitor them. Alternatively, the teacher could set up the situation with the whole class then, by prompting the students, get suggestions as to what A and B might say to each other.

Whichever method is chosen, it is essential that the students know *exactly* what they have to do before they are allowed to begin.

4 Working through an activity

It is probably better if all pairs start working at the same time rather than working one after the other. During the activity, the teacher moves from pair to pair, as a passive observer, noting problems or mistakes which can be taken up with the whole group afterwards.

The length of the activities varies from approximately five to twenty minutes. It is up to the teacher and the class to decide whether to spend a whole lesson on the activities or else to make them a part of the normal lesson. (Perhaps a combination of these two is a good idea.)

Finally, since not all groups will finish at exactly the same time, it may be necessary for the teacher to have a definite 'finishing time' in mind for some of the more open-ended activities.

5 Following up an activity

The teacher should always spend a few minutes after an activity discussing it with the class. The discussion could include talking about what the students found difficult as well as finding out if anyone wanted to say something but didn't have the necessary language to express himself or herself. This is also the time when any mistakes can be pointed out and, if necessary, revision practice given.

Finally, it is a good idea occasionally to ask one of the pairs to practise the activity again while the rest of the class listen and monitor their performance.

6 Activity 1 and Activity 2

Although these two activities practise asking and answering questions, the chief reason for putting them first in the book is that they are a useful way of breaking the ice when the class is a new one – although they are still useful even when the class has been together for some time.

1 Getting to know you (1)

Get to know something about Student A by asking him/her questions and filling in the following form. (Student A will also ask you questions.)

Name: .... Date of birth: ....
(day) (month) (year)

Place of birth: Town: .... Country: ....

Nationality: ....

Home town/village: ....

Number of people in family: ....

Mother	Father	Number of brothers	Number of sisters	Anyone else
☐	☐	....	....	....

Father's name: .... Age: ....

Mother's name: .... Age: ....

Still at school   Yes/No   Left school: .... (year)

(If Student A has left school):

Present job: ....

or

College/University: ....

Started learning English: .... (year)

Interests: ....
....

Favourite pop singer: ....

Languages spoken (apart from English): ....
....

Main ambition: ....

Before starting, work out which questions to ask. For example:

What's your name?
When were you born?
Where were you born?
Have you got any sisters?
When did you start learning English?

When you have finished, use the answers Student A gave you to fill in the gaps in the following sentences:

1 I spoke to ....

2 He/She was born on .... , 19...... in ....
(*town/village*) in .... (*country*).

3 He/She is .... (*nationality*) and lives in a town/village called
....

4 There are ...... people altogether in his/her family – his/her ....
....

5 His/Her father is called .... and he is .... years old.

6 His/Her mother's name is .... and she is .... (*age*).

7 He/She is still at school.

OR He/She left school in 19...... and is now studying at ....
.... (*name of College/University*)

OR He/She left school in 19...... and is now working.
He/She is a/an ....

8 He/She started learning English in 19......

9 His/Her interests are ....
.... and his/her favourite pop singer
is ....

10 Apart from English, he/she also speaks ....

11 Finally, his/her main ambition is to ....
....

When you have finished, find another partner. Now tell this person all about Student A by reading out the sentences above.

2 Getting to know you (2)

Ask Student A questions to find out the things below. Before starting, work out which questions to ask. (Student A will also ask you questions.)

Find out if Student A:	Yes	No	Other Information
1 is afraid of flying. (Are you . . .?)			
2 is the tallest person in his/her family. (If the answer is No, find out who is the tallest person in Student A's family)			
3 is good at mathematics.			
4 lives in a house or a flat. (Do you . . .?)			
5 reads a newspaper every day.			
6 gets up before 7 o'clock.			
7 has got a bicycle. (Have you got . . .?)			
8 has got more than one Christian name. (If the answer is Yes, find out what other Christian names Student A has got)			
9 has got a telephone. (If the answer is Yes, find out Student A's telephone number)			
10 can type. (Can you . . .?)			
11 can play a musical instrument. (If the answer is Yes, find out which musical instrument Student A can play)			
12 was born in a town or a village. (Were you . . .?)			
13 watched television last night. (Did you . . .?)			
14 went abroad last summer. (If the answer is Yes, find out where Student A went)			
15 has been to Paris. (Have you . . .?)			
16 has read any books by Agatha Christie.			
17 is going somewhere this weekend. (If the answer is Yes, find out where Student A is going) (Are you going . . .?)			
18 would like to be a film-star or a pop star. (Would you . . .?)			

When you have finished, find another partner. Now tell him/her what you found out about Student A.

3 Missing information: the Eurovision Song Contest

A daily newspaper is publishing each day a short description of some of the singers taking part in the Eurovision Song Contest. Here is today's list of singers. Unfortunately, some of the information about them is missing. Ask Student A questions to find out the missing information and fill it in. (Student A also has missing information and will ask you questions.)

You can ask questions like these:

> How old is . . . (say name)?
> Where does . . . (say name) . . . live?
> Which country is . . . (say name) . . . singing for?
> Is . . . (say name) . . . married or single?
> How long has . . . (say name) . . . been a pop singer?
> What are . . . (say name)'s interests?
> What is the name of the song . . . (say name) . . . is going to sing?
> What is . . . (say name)'s ambition?

Who's who in the Eurovision Song Contest   Part 2

Name	Maria Rossi		Astrid Klempe	
Age			22	
Home town	Milan			
Country	Italy			
Married/single			single	
Length of time as a pop singer	8 years		4 years	
Interests	music golf painting		swimming	
Song title (in English)			Strange Love	
Ambition	To buy a Rolls-Royce			

Name	Fleming Larsen		Paula Allen	
Age			19	
Home town			Dublin	
Country	Denmark		Ireland	
Married/single	single			
Length of time as a pop singer	6 years			
Interests	football reading fishing		.... cooking	
Song title (in English)			When You Are Gone	
Ambition	To sing in the U.S.A.			

Name	'Nana'		Marcel Meyer	
Age			34	
Home town	Athens			
Country	Greece		France	
Married/single			married	
Length of time as a pop singer			12 years	
Interests	tennis .... travelling		karate	
Song title (in English)	Love Me Tonight			
Ambition			To write a musical	

When you have finished, check with Student A to see if you have filled in the missing information correctly.

(NOTE: The Eurovision Song Contest is a competition held once a year by the various television companies in Europe to pick the best pop song. There is a jury in each country who give marks for each song and the song with the highest total is the winner. The competitors from each country must sing the song in the language of that country.)

4 Questionnaire: likes and dislikes

Work on your own. Read through the following sentences and choose an answer (I like, I quite like, I don't like, I hate, etc.). Mark your answer with a cross (×).

I love	I like	I quite like	I don't really like	I don't like	I hate	
						listening to pop music.
						cats.
						writing letters.
						horror films (*Dracula, Frankenstein*, etc.).
						this town.
						being alone.
						cooking.
						ice-cream.
						the smell of garlic.
						singing.
						modern furniture.
						watching football.
						washing my hair.
						our teacher.
						flying.
						my school (or my job).
						getting up early.
						going to discos.
						visiting relatives.
						talking about myself.

When you have finished, find a partner (Student A). Now talk about your likes and dislikes like this:

You:	I hate cooking.	
Student A:	Yes, so do I/Yes, me too. OR Oh, I don't. (I quite like it.)	

Student A:	I don't like horror films.	
You:	No, neither do I.	OR Oh, I do. (I love them.)

Take it in turns to start.

5   Who's who?

Here are six people plus some information about them:

18

Sally is the youngest.
Peter is taller than Mary but shorter than Mike.
Mary is fatter than both Sally and Julie.
Julie's hair is longer than Sally's.
The thinnest person is only 16.

Student A also has information about the six people. Work together to see if you can work out their names and their ages. (Write them in the boxes.)

You are allowed to read out the information you have about the six people *but you must not let Student A see your book.*

6 One-sided dialogue: making suggestions

Student A is your friend. Today is Friday. You are discussing where to go tomorrow. Unfortunately, you can see only your part of the dialogue so you must listen very carefully to what Student A says. Use the *Saturday Guide* on the opposite page when trying to decide where to go.

Before you start, read through your part to have some idea of what you will say. When you are both ready you can begin.

Student A: . . .

You: Yes, all right. What do you suggest?

Student A: . . .

You: Well, let's see . . . Ah! This sounds interesting!

Student A: . . .

You: (*Read something out of the section of the* Saturday Guide *marked* SPORTS EVENTS)

Student A: . . .

You: All right. How about . . . (*suggest going on an excursion from the* Saturday Guide)

Student A: . . .

You: Well, there are two here – one to . . . (*explain where the excursions are going to*)

Student A: . . .

You: Well you suggest something, then.

Student A: . . .

You: It depends on what sort of an exhibition it is.

Student A: . . .

You: No, they don't sound very interesting.

Student A: . . .

You: I know! Let's go to . . . (*suggest something from the section marked* OTHER EVENTS)

Student A: . . .

You: (*Answer*) And it only costs . . . (*say what it costs*)

Student A: . . .

You: Great!

SATURDAY GUIDE

Sports Events

Indoor Football

Finals of the South of England indoor football competition for schools.
Leisure Centre
Kick-off: 10.30
Final: approx. 4.15

Admission 50p

Water-polo

International match between England and Wales.

Lansdown swimming baths 2 p.m.–5 p.m.

Admission £1

Judo

National championships for women.

Wigmore Sports Centre 1.30–4.30

Admission 60p

Exhibitions

18th-century Landscape Paintings

Exhibition of eighteenth-century landscape paintings by well-known local artists.

Grover Art Gallery 10–5.30

Admission 80p

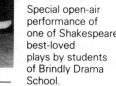

Scandinavian Design

Exhibition of modern furniture from Denmark, Sweden and Finland.

Design Centre 9.30–4.30

Admission Free

Excursions

Isle of Wight and Stonehenge

Coach tour to the Isle of Wight and Stonehenge.
Depart: 7.30 from Station Road.
Arrive back: approx. 9.30 p.m.
Cost £2.50
(including lunch)

The Motor Show

Special coach trip to the Motor Show at Earls Court, London.
Depart: 9.15 from Station Road.
Arrive back: approx. 8.15 p.m.

Cost £4.50
(including lunch and admission)

Other Events

A Midsummer Night's Dream

Special open-air performance of one of Shakespeare's best-loved plays by students of Brindly Drama School.

Singleton Park 2.30 p.m.

Seats £1.50

Cat Show

Local cat show at St Peter's Church Hall. 9.30–5.30

Admission 20p

Computer Fair

See and try out the latest in home computers. Special attraction for children – Games Corner – a chance to play the latest computer games.

Wigmore Conference Centre 10–6 p.m.

Admission adults £1 children 50p

7 Following instructions (1)

On the opposite page is a rectangle which contains twenty squares. Before you start, fill in the following:

1 In square number 7 write today's date.
2 In square number 12 write which year it is.
3 In square number 13 write which day it was yesterday.
4 In square number 16 write your teacher's name.
5 In square number 17 write the number 42.
6 In square number 19 write the colour of your eyes.
7 In square number 20 write your name.

Now work with Student A. He/she has a large rectangle in his/her book similar to yours. But all twenty squares are empty. Help him/her to fill them in by reading out loud the following instructions. *But do not let Student A see your book.*

When you have finished, compare rectangles to see if Student A has filled in everything correctly.

Here are the instructions:

1 Start in the black square. Go up one square. Draw a picture of the sun in this square.
2 Go right two squares. Draw a picture of a house in this square.
3 Go down two squares. In this square write which day it was yesterday.
4 Go left two squares, then down one square. In this square write our teacher's name.
5 Go back to the square with the drawing of the sun. Go right three squares. In this square draw a triangle.
6 Go down two squares. Draw a picture of a cup in this square.
7 Go left two squares, then up one square. In this square write today's date.
8 In the square above this, draw a picture of a horse.
9 Go back to the square with the drawing of a cup. In the square below this write down what colour my eyes are.
10 Go left three squares, then up one square. In this square draw a picture of a tree.
11 Go to the square below the drawing of the house. In this square draw a large cross.
12 Go right two squares. In this square draw a large circle.
13 Go down two squares. In this square write my name.
14 Go left three squares. Multiply seven by six, then write your answer in this square.
15 Finally, write in the square to the right of the drawing of the tree which year it is now.

1	2	3	4	5
6	7	8	9	10
11	12	13	14	15
16	17	18	19	20

8 Missing information: flats and houses

Ask Student A questions to find out the missing information about the house and the flat in the table below. (Student A also has missing information and will ask you questions.)

Before you start, work out which questions to ask. For example:

> Where's (*the flat*)?
> Is (*the house*) big?
> How many rooms are there in (*the flat*)? What are they?
> Has (*the flat*) got central heating?
> How much is the rent for (*the house*)?
> Is there anything else you can tell me about (*the flat*)?

	FLAT		HOUSE	
Street			Park Road	
Size	big	☑	big	☐
	quite big	☐	quite big	☐
	small	☐	small	☐
Condition	modern	☐	modern	☐
	quite modern	☐	quite modern	☐
	not very modern	☐	not very modern	☑
Number of rooms			*downstairs* two *upstairs* three	
List of rooms			a living-room a kitchen 2 bedrooms a bathroom/toilet	
Central heating			No	
Near the shops	Yes			
Distance from town centre			2 miles	
Rent	£40 a week			
Any other information			Large garden. Garage.	

When you are ready, take it in turns to ask and answer questions. When you have finished, compare your tables.

9 Following instructions (2)

Here is a rectangle which contains twenty squares. You are going to write or draw something in fifteen of them. Student A will tell you what to draw or write and in which squares. But it is not as easy as it sounds, so you will have to listen very carefully to his/her instructions.

1	2	3	4
5	6	7	8
9	■ 10	11	12
13	14	15	16
17	18	19	20

Before you start, make sure you have a pencil ready. If, at any time, you do not understand what Student A says, you can ask him/her to repeat the instructions (e.g. I'm sorry, I didn't understand that. Could you say it again, please?). *But you are not allowed to ask for the number of the square you are to draw or write in.*

When you have finished, compare your rectangle with Student A's to see if you have filled in everything correctly.

10 This is my boyfriend/girlfriend

Student A is your cousin. He/she has got a new girlfriend/boyfriend. Find out all you can about him/her by asking Student A questions, such as:

What's his/her name?
How old is he/she?
Where did you meet him/her?
What does he/she do?
Have your parents met him/her?

Try to think of at least fifteen questions to ask.
When you are both ready, Student A will begin.

11 Newspaper interview (1)

Your name is Brian (or Jane) White.
 You are a journalist. You work for the *Daily News*.
You are in Sweden to interview Maria (or Rolf) Lells (Student A). She/he
is the leader of a group of people who are going on a Peace March from
Stockholm to London.
 Before you start, work out some questions to ask. For example:

> When are you starting your march?
> When do you hope to arrive in London?
> Are you visiting many countries on the way?
> What are you going to do when you get to London?
> What will you do about food?
> How many people are marching with you?

Try to think of other questions to ask.
 When you are both ready, you can begin. You can start like this:

> How do you do, Mr/Miss Lells. My name's ....
> of the *Daily News*.
> May I ask you one or two questions about the march?

And you can finish:

> Thank you very much for answering my questions, and good luck
> with the march.

12 This is my brother

On the opposite page is a photograph of your brother and his family. Student A is a new friend you have met on holiday. You are going to tell him/her all about your brother and his family.

Before you start, think of the following:

> your brother's name/age/job
> his wife's name/job
> their children's names/ages
> where they live
> how long they have been married
> how often you see them
> what your brother's like (kind, friendly, funny, etc.)
> his interests

When you are both ready, you can begin like this:

> Would you like to see a photograph of my brother and his family?

(NOTE: Student A will probably ask you lots of questions, so be prepared to use your imagination!)

13 Questionnaire: habits and daily routines

Find out something about Student A's habits and daily routine by asking him/her questions. (Student A will also ask you questions.)

Before you start, work out which questions to ask. Then take it in turns to ask and answer questions. Mark Student A's answers with a cross (×).

Find out if Student A:	Yes, always	Yes, usually	Yes, often	Yes, sometimes	No, not often	No, not usually	No, hardly ever	No, never
gets up before 7.30 (Do you ever get . . . ?)								
gets all his/her homework right (Do you ever get all your . . . ?)								
has a party on his/her birthday								
goes abroad in the summer								
watches television in the evenings								
gets a suntan in the summer								
remembers people's birthdays								
feels shy when he/she meets new people								
drinks tea with milk								
eats three meals a day								
walks to school (or work)								
feels bored in class								
hears alarm clocks								
makes his/her bed before going out in the morning								
bites his/her nails when he/she is nervous								

When you have finished, use the answers Student A gave you to fill in the missing words in the following sentences. (Remember: If Student A answered No, not often or No, not usually, you write, *'He/she doesn't often/usually . . .'*)

I spoke to .... (*name*)

1 He/She .... gets up before 7.30.

2 He/She .... gets all his/her homework right.

3 He/She .... has a party on his/her birthday.

4 He/She .... goes abroad in the summer.

5 He/She .... watches television in the evenings.

6 He/She .... gets a suntan in the summer.

7 He/She .... remembers people's birthdays.

8 He/She .... feels shy when he/she meets new people.

9 He/She .... drinks tea with milk.

10 He/She .... eats three meals a day.

11 He/She .... walks to school/work.

12 He/She .... feels bored in class.

13 He/She .... hears alarm clocks.

14 He/She .... makes his/her bed before
going out in the morning.

15 He/She .... bites his/her nails when he/she
is nervous.

14 For sale

You want to buy a second-hand stereo cassette recorder. You see the following advertisement in the newspaper and decide to phone up about it. (Student A is the person who is selling the recorder.)

FOR SALE

Stereo cassette recorder.
Only three years old.
Reasonable price.

Phone 347299

Before you start, work out some questions to ask. For example:

What make is it?
How much do you want for it?
Does it have a radio?

Here are some other things you can ask about:

- if it has a clock
- if you can record directly from the radio
- how powerful the speakers are
- if the recorder has a pause button
- how big it is
    etc.

Finally, if you are interested in buying it, try to arrange a day and time when you can go and see it.

When Student A answers the phone, you can begin:

Good (*morning*). I'm phoning about your advertisement in today's paper. You haven't sold the cassette recorder yet, I hope?

---

15 Eye-witness

You work in a shop. Here is a photograph of a man who came into your shop this morning. Look at the photograph for 2–3 minutes. Try to remember as many details about him as you can. *But you must not write anything down on paper.*

When you have finished, turn over to the next page.

The man who came into your shop this morning stole something when you were answering the telephone. You have phoned the police station to report him. A policeman/policewoman (Student A) is going to interview you about the man. Try to answer his/her questions *without looking back at the photograph*.

Student A will begin.

16 Complete the crossword

The crossword on the opposite page is only half filled in. Student A also has a crossword that is only half filled in. Take it in turns to ask what the missing words are and to answer by trying to explain each word. For example:

Student A asks:	You answer:
What's 15 across?	It's a place you go to when you want to borrow books.
What's 7 down?	You go here when you want to catch a train.

Before you start, work out ways of explaining the words already filled in. If you guess a word correctly but are not sure how to spell it, you can ask Student A to spell it for you.

When you have finished, compare your crosswords.

DOWN

ACROSS

										¹S↓
										A
				¹→		²↓				L
										T
		²→	³T↓	A	L	Y			
	⁴↓		H						
³→E	L	V	U	S			⁵B↓	
			R			A	
⁴→			S			N
			D			K
	⁶↓	A		
⁵→H	A	P	P	Y
⁷S↓				⁶→B	E	⁸D↓		⁹S↓
⁷→T						I		C
A	⁸→					¹⁰↓E		H
⁹→			T					O
			I					O
¹⁰→		¹¹↓	O		¹¹→			L
			N
¹²↓	¹²→S	N	O	W	¹³→W	A	R
¹⁴→S	H	O	E	¹³S↓
				¹⁴↓
¹⁵→L	I	B	R	A	R	Y
		¹⁶→J	A	P	A	N

ACROSS: SALT, ITALY, ELVIS, HAPPY, BED, SNOW, WAR, SHOES, LIBRARY, JAPAN

DOWN: THURSDAY, BANK, STATION, SCHOOL

(Based on an idea by
Elizabeth Woodeson
in *MET*, Vol. 10, 1982)

17 Carry on talking

Situation 1

Here are the opening words of a conversation between two friends:

> A: You look happy, . . . (*say name*).
> B: Yes, I am. I had such a wonderful time last night.

Using these words, you are going to continue the conversation with Student A. (You will take the part of A.)
Before you start, think of what you might say. For example:

> Where did Student A go last night?
> Was he/she with someone?
> What did he/she do?

Try to keep the conversation going for as long as you can. You start.

Situation 2

Here are the opening words of another conversation between two friends:

> A: What happened to you last night? Why weren't you at the party?
> B: I'm sorry, . . . (*say name*), but there was trouble at home so I couldn't go.

This time, you are going to take the part of B.
Before you start, think of what you might say. For example:

> What was the trouble at home?
> Why didn't you phone Student A to let him/her know you wouldn't be at the party?
> What was the party like? Who was there?

When you are both ready, you can begin. Student A starts.

Way Out Weekend Courses This month's courses

Computer programming

Dates: 2nd, 3rd   *Days*: Fri–Sat.

Computer programming course for complete beginners at Wilton College, Manchester. Learn how to write your own programs in Basic. One computer per person.

Course leader: David Chip, Head of Computer Studies, Wilton College

Maximum number on course: 15

Accommodation: Central Hotel (5 minutes from the College)

Cost: £190

Bird-watching

Dates: 9th, 10th   *Days*: Fri–Sat.

Spend the weekend bird-watching (mainly sea birds) in West Wales. Cameras and binoculars may be hired for £10 a day.

Course leader: David Atkins, author of several books on bird-watching

Maximum number on course: 12

Accommodation: Grand Hotel, Tenby

Cost: £180

Folk dancing

Dates: 23rd–25th   *Days*: Fri–Sun.

A weekend for people who love folk dancing. Practise old dances, learn new ones. All in the pleasant atmosphere of the Richmond Conference Centre on the Isle of Wight.

Course leader: Rosemary Morris, author of *Traditional British Folk Dances*

Maximum number on course: 40

Accommodation: at the Centre

Cost: £200

Self-hypnosis

Dates: 2nd–4th   *Days*: Fri–Sun.

Learn how to hypnotize yourself at Barnet Manor, Cambridge, under the direction of one of America's leading hypnotists. See how self-hypnosis can help you to relax, overcome fears, give up bad habits, etc.

Course leader: Dr Henry Bond, author of the best-selling book *Change Your Life Through Self-Hypnosis*

Maximum number on course: 12

Accommodation: at the Manor

Cost: £350

Water-colour painting

Dates: 23rd–25th   *Days*: Fri–Sun.

Learn how to paint in watercolours among the lakes and mountains of the Lake District. Paints and other materials supplied.

Course leader: Amanda Turner, painter and Art teacher

Maximum number on course: 12

Accommodation: Lake View Hotel, Penrith

Cost: £250

Pottery

Dates: 16th, 17th   *Days*: Fri–Sat.

Pottery weekend for beginners at the Gilbert School of Art in Bristol. You will learn how to make pots both by hand and on a wheel. All materials supplied.

Course leader: Margaret Clay, Pottery teacher at the Gilbert School of Art

Maximum number on course: 15

Accommodation: Station Hotel (10 minutes from the School)

Cost: £185

Weaving

Dates: 27th, 28th   *Days*: Sat–Sun.

Weaving course for absolute beginners at Glebe House, Brighton. One loom per person.

Course leader: Pamela Dobson, teacher

Maximum number on course: 10

Accommodation: at Glebe House

Cost: £165

Ghost hunting

Dates: 16th–18th *Days*: Fri–Sun.

A weekend for those who like something different at London House, Yorkshire. Lectures and talks by various experts on ghosts, and the course includes spending the night at a 'haunted house'. Not recommended for people with weak hearts.

Course leader: Dr Roger Spook, author of *Haunted Houses in Britain*

Maximum number on course: 15

Accommodation: at London House

Cost: £175

20 Complete the drawing (1)

On the opposite page is a drawing of a kitchen. Under the drawing are a number of things which are found in a kitchen (knives, forks, a clock, etc.) Student A is going to tell you where these things go. When he/she tells you, draw the object(s) in the correct place. You are allowed to ask questions but you *must not look at Student A's drawing*.

When you have finished, compare your drawings.

You can ask questions like these:

Where's the clock?
Where are the glasses?

Here are some other questions you might ask:

I didn't understand that. Could you say it again, please?
Do you mean here?
In which cupboard – the one on the left or the one on the right?
Is it on the bottom shelf or on the top shelf?

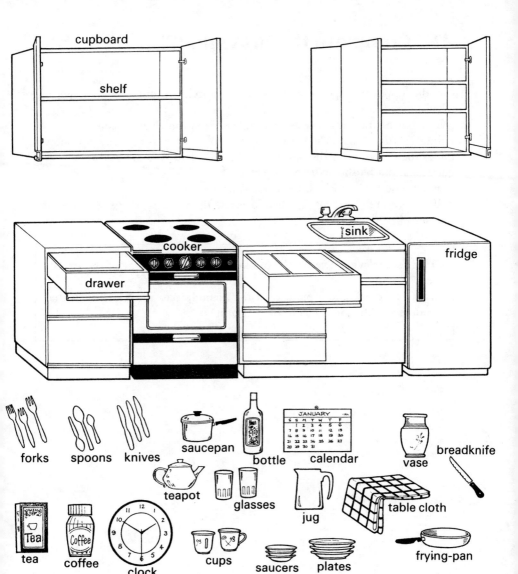

cupboard

shelf

cooker

sink

fridge

drawer

forks spoons knives saucepan bottle calendar vase breadknife

teapot glasses jug table cloth

tea coffee clock cups saucers plates frying-pan

21 Complete the drawing (2)

On the opposite page is a drawing of a living-room complete with a television set, a radio, a cat, etc. Student A also has a drawing of a living-room, but his/her drawing is incomplete. Help him/her to complete it by telling him/her where the various things go. (The missing items are shown under the drawing on the opposite page.) Student A is allowed to ask you questions, but he/she *must not see your book*.

When you have finished, compare your drawings.

When you tell Student A where to draw the various things, you can use phrases like these:

> There's a television set in the bookcase. It's on the right of the stereo set.
> There's a clock and a picture on the mantelpiece. The clock is in the middle and the picture is to the left of it.

bookcase

shelf

mantelpiece

coffee table

armchair

sofa

cat

picture

ashtray

spot light

magazine

clock

painting

glasses

box of matches

vase of flowers

bottle

cushion

vases

poster

television set

radio

lamp

book

22 Missing information: the life of Elvis Presley

A pop magazine has just started a new series called 'The History of Rock 'n' Roll'. Each week it presents a short life-history of a famous rock 'n' roll singer. On the opposite page is the life-history of this week's star – Elvis Presley. Unfortunately, some of the information about him is missing. By asking Student A questions, fill in the missing information. (Student A also has missing information and will ask you questions.)

Before you start, read through the life of Elvis on the opposite page and work out which questions to ask. For example:

> When was he born?
> Where did he move to in 1948?
> When did he leave school?
> Who did he meet in 1955?
> What happened in 1972?

When you are both ready you can begin. Take it in turns to ask and answer questions. *But you must not let Student A see your book.*

When you have finished, check to see if you have filled in everything correctly.

38

Full name: Elvis Aaron Presley
Parents: Vernon and Gladys Presley

Brothers/sisters: Jesse Garon (twin brother) Died ....

Year	Main event(s)
1935	Born in Tupelo, Mississipi, on ....
1942	Got a guitar from his father for his birthday.
1948	Moved to ...., Tennessee. Started at a new school. His father bought him a new guitar.
. . .	Left school and got a job as a driver with the Crown Electrical Company. That summer, he went along to Sun Records in Memphis and paid $......... to record two songs for his mother's birthday.
1954	Sam Phillips, the owner of Sun Records, asked Elvis to record a song called 'That's All Right'. .... people bought the record.
1955	Met Colonel .... He became Elvis's manager.
1956	Recorded a song called 'Heartbreak Hotel'. It sold over a million copies.
1957	Made more records – all of them were big hits. Became known as the 'King of Rock 'n' Roll'. He bought a big house in Memphis which he called Graceland. Also went to .... to make his first film – *Love Me Tender*.
1958	Went into the army and became a soldier in West Germany. On August 18th, his mother died.
. . .	Left the army and went back to Hollywood to make more films.
1967	Got married to Priscilla Beaumont – a girl he had first met when he was a soldier in Germany.
1968	Appeared on a special television show. His daughter, ..., was born.
1972	....
1973	Elvis and Priscilla got divorced.
. . .	Died of a heart attack at the age of 42 on August 16th. He left all his money to his daughter. .... people turned up for his funeral and his records were played on the radio all day.
1978	100 million Elvis LPs were sold. The 'King of Rock 'n' Roll' was dead but certainly not forgotten.

23 Looking at holiday photographs (1)

Student A is going to show you some photographs he/she took while on holiday last summer. Try to ask lots of questions about them, as well as questions about the holiday itself.

Here are some questions you can ask (think of others):

(a) *about the photographs*:

Where was this taken?
What's that building there?
Who are these people? Do you know them?

(b) *about the holiday*:

How long did you stay in . . . ?
Was it nice there?
Who did you go with?
Where did you stay?
What did you do?

Try to think of other questions.

When Student A asks you if you would like to look at some holiday photographs you can say:

Yes, please. I love looking at photographs.

When you have seen the photographs, you can say:

Thanks for letting me see the photographs.
They were really interesting.

24 Newspaper interview (2)

You are Paul (or Cathy) Storm.

You are the manager of the American all-female pop group, Cheese. Next month you start your European tour. You are in London at the moment making all the final arrangements. Here is a list of the dates and places the group will be playing at during the tour:

Date	Town	Country
2nd	Manchester	England
4th	Amsterdam	Holland
5th	Brussels	Belgium
7th, 8th	Hamburg	West Germany
10th	Copenhagen	Denmark
12th	Göteborg	Sweden
15th	Helsinki	Finland
16th, 17th	Paris	France
20th, 21st	London	England

Cheese became really famous just over a year ago with the song 'Wild Woman', which sold over three million records. While you are in Europe you hope to record a new single. You are also planning to do television shows in England and in West Germany. You hope after this tour that Cheese will be as popular in Europe as they are in the United States.

Student A is a journalist. He/she is going to interview you about your European tour. (Be ready to use your imagination!)

25 Looking at holiday photographs (2)

The photographs on the opposite page are ones you took when you were on holiday last summer. You are going to show them to Student A. Talk to him/her about the photographs and about your holiday.

Before you start, think about the following:

(a) the photographs: where the photographs were taken the name of the building/place who the people are	*(b) the holiday*: where you went how long you stayed there who you went with what you did there what the weather was like

Ask as many questions as you can.

When you are ready, you can begin. Start like this:

> Would you like to see some photographs of
> my holiday in .... ?

Then show the photographs to Student A.

26 One-sided dialogue: shopping

Read the following dialogue with Student A.

Because you can see only your part, you must listen very carefully to what Student A says. Use the drawing of the shop on the opposite page. Also, when Student A buys something, make a note of how much it costs.

Before you start, read through your part to have some idea of what you will say. When you are both ready you can begin.

Student A: ...
You: Certainly. Anything else?
Student A: ...
You: (*Ask Student A if he/she wants a large packet or a small packet*)
Student A: ...
You: (*Answer*)
Student A: ...
You: How many?
Student A: ...
You: Anything else?
Student A: ...
You: Grade 1 or Grade 3?
Student A: ...
You: (*Say what they cost*)
Student A: ...
You Yes, of course. Large or small?
Student A: ...
You: (*Answer*) Anything else?
Student A: ...
You: What sort?
Student A: ...
You: (*Name the four sorts of coffee you have got*)
Student A: ...
You: (*Answer. Say how much it costs*)
Student A: ...
You: Right. Is that all?
Student A: ...
You: I'm afraid we've only got ... (*Name what sort of cheese you have got*)
Student A: ...
You: Er ... let's see now ... (*Add up the prices and tell Student A what it comes to altogether*)
    Student A gives you £10
You: Thank you. And ... change. (*Give Student A the change from £10*)
Student A: ...
You: (*Answer*)

TOMATO SOUP	CORNFLAKES	TEA	SUGAR
large 60p	large pkt 70p	35p	50p
small 25p	small pkt 50p		

BISCUITS
30p

CRISPS
50p

COFFEE
BRAZIL £1.50p
MARTIN HOUSE 95p
BLEND £1.20p
NESCO £1.10p

Edam
£1.50

Danish
Blue
£1.20

CHEESE	BUTTER	MARGARINE	MILK	EGGS	
	50p	25p	20p/pint	grade 1	grade 3
				90p doz	80p doz

APPLES	BANANAS	POTATOES
40p/lb	40p/lb	15p/lb

40p/lb = 40 pence per pound
1 lb = approximately 0.5 kilograms)

27 Where's the station?

Look at the map on the opposite page. There are ten buildings which have not been marked. They are the following:

the police station	the record shop	the hospital
the library	the bank	the disco
the school	the grocer's	the drugstore
the fire station		

Student A knows where these buildings are. Ask him/her questions to find out. When you know, mark them on the map. (Student A also has missing buildings and will ask you questions.)

(NOTE: The six buildings marked in black are on both maps, so if Student A asks you where the baker's is, you can answer: 'It's in Penny Lane, opposite the boutique.')

When you have finished, compare your maps to check that you have filled in all the missing buildings correctly.

Take it in turns to ask and answer questions. (Ask: Where's the . . . ?)

When you answer, you can use sentences like these:

It's in (*Green Road*)	next to the . . .
	opposite the . . .
	between the . . . and the . . .

It's the (*first/second/etc.*) building on the (*right/left*) in (*Penny Lane*).

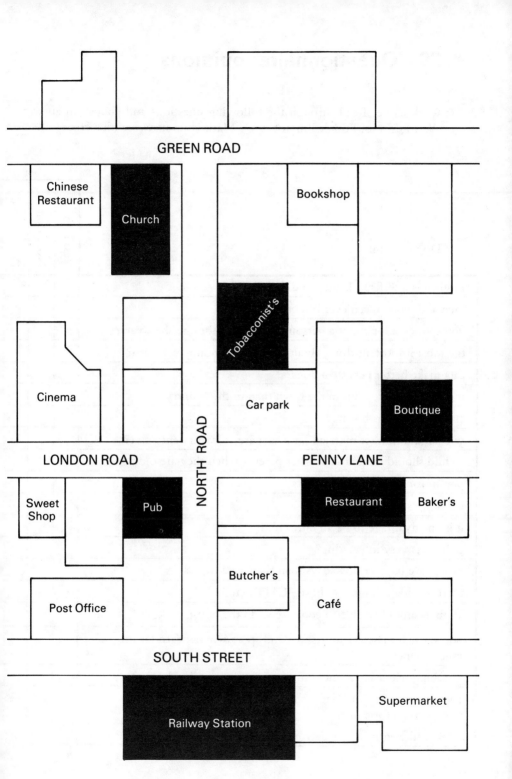

GREEN ROAD

Chinese Restaurant

Church

Bookshop

Cinema

Tobacconist's

Car park

Boutique

LONDON ROAD

PENNY LANE

NORTH ROAD

Sweet Shop

Pub

Restaurant

Baker's

Butcher's

Post Office

Café

SOUTH STREET

Railway Station

Supermarket

28 Questionnaire: opinions

Work alone. Read through the following questions and choose an answer (Yes, I do/No, I don't/I'm not sure). Mark your answer with a cross (×).

Do you think . . .

	Yes, I do	No, I don't	I'm not sure
English is a difficult language to learn?			
men and women can ever be equal?			
you can tell a lot about a person from the clothes he/she wears?			
the most important thing about a job is the money you earn?			
cats make better pets than dogs?			
it is better to grow up in the town than in the country?			
classical music is boring?			
you should not get married until you are at least twenty-five?			
a child should look after his/her parents when they are old?			
pop music is only for teenagers?			
smoking should be banned?			
it is an advantage to be an only child?			
politics is very interesting?			
people are happier nowadays than they used to be?			
there are such things as ghosts, UFOs, etc.?			
all men should be able to cook, sew, do the housework, and so on?			
pop stars, film-stars, sportsmen and sportswomen earn far too much money?			
watching television is more interesting than reading books?			
getting married and having children is more important for a woman than for a man?			
there will ever be a Third World War?			

When you have finished, work with Student A. Take it in turns to ask each other's opinions and to agree or disagree with them. Ask questions like these:

A: Do you think English is a difficult language to learn?
B: Yes, I do.
A: Yes, so do I. OR Do you? I don't. I think . . . . .

B: Do you think politics is very interesting?
A: No, I don't.
B: No, neither do I. OR Don't you? I do. I think . . . . .

A: Do you think men and women can ever be equal?
B: I'm not sure, really.
A: Oh, I do. OR Oh, I don't. OR No, neither am I.

(NOTE: If you disagree with Student A, try to give a reason for your opinion.)

29 Asking for information about a tour

You are a clerk at the London Travel Information Centre at Victoria Coach Station. Student A phones you up about your day tours. Help him/her to find something suitable.

Here are tomorrow's tours:

Tour to:	Departure	Return	Fare	No. of seats left
London sightseeing tour	9.30	16.00	£15.00*	1
Windsor Castle and Hampton Court	12.30	17.30	£13.50	3
Brighton	8.30	19.30	£20.00*	2
Isle of Wight	8.45	20.00	£23.50*	7
Oxford	9.00	16.30	£16.50*	4
Bristol Zoo	7.45	19.45	£25.00	5
Note: all tours leave from Victoria Coach Station			* includes lunch	

If Student A wishes to book seats for one of the tours, fill in the following booking form:

BOOKING FORM	Day Tours

Name: ....

Tour: ....

No. of seats: ....   Cost: £ ....

Also tell him/her that he/she can pick up the tickets tomorrow morning at Victoria Coach Station.

You can begin like this:

Good (*morning*). London Travel Information Centre.

30 Asking for information about summer jobs

You are a student. You would like to work during the summer for about 4–6 weeks. You can start any time after June 1st. You see the following advertisement in the newspaper and decide to phone up for more information. (Student A works at Summer Jobs Agency.)

LOOKING FOR A JOB THIS SUMMER?

We can put you in touch with the right people.
For further information telephone
SUMMER JOBS AGENCY
01–210–8007

If any of the jobs sound interesting, make a note of the following:

Job: ....

Place: ....

Starting date: ....

Length: ....

Salary: ....

Person to contact: ....

Tel. No.: ....

When Student A answers the phone, you can begin:

Good (*afternoon*). I'd like some information about summer jobs. What sort of jobs have you got, please?

---

31 One-sided dialogue: an invitation

Read the following dialogue with Student A.

Because you can see only your part, you must listen very carefully to what Student A says. Use the diary on the opposite page.

Before you start, read through your part to work out what you will say. When you are both ready, you can begin.

Student A: . . .

You: Hello, . . . (*say Student A's name*). It's me – . . . (*say your name*).

Student A: . . .

You: (*Answer*) And you?

Student A: . . .

You: Listen, would you like to . . . (*invite Student A to go to the cinema with you next week*)

Student A: . . .

You: How about . . . (*suggest either Tuesday or Wednesday*)

Student A: . . .

You: Yes, . . . (*repeat day*) would be fine.

Student A: . . .

You: (*Suggest a time*)

Student A: . . .

You: (*Suggest a place to meet*)

Student A: . . .

You: Right. Well, I'll see you on . . . (*the day you arranged*), then.

Student A: . . .

You: Good. 'Bye for now, then.

Student A: . . .

Fill in your diary: Go to cinema with . . . Meet at . . . (*time/place*)

Your diary next week (evenings)

MONDAY

Go for a meal with John and Simon 19⁰⁰

TUESDAY

WEDNESDAY

THURSDAY

FRIDAY

Appendix: Guide to the structures and functions used

Activity 1: Getting to know you (1)

Type of activity
Ice-breaker

Main structures
Present Simple – question and answer forms
Verbs: to be, have got, various others

Examples:
What's your name?
Have you got any brothers?
Where do you come from?

Main functions
Asking for and giving personal information
(see above examples)

Activity 2: Getting to know you (2)

Type of activity
Ice-breaker

Main structures
Various tenses – question and answer forms, including short forms (Yes, I am/No, I'm not, Yes, I do/No, I don't, etc.)

Examples:

Are you afraid of the dark?	Yes, I am/No, I'm not
Do you live in a town or a village?	(I live) in . . .
Have you got more than two brothers?	Yes, I have/No, I haven't
Can you swim?	Yes, I can/No, I can't
Were you born in May?	Yes, I was/No, I wasn't
Did you listen to the radio last night?	Yes, I did/No, I didn't
etc.	

Main functions
Asking and answering questions about yourself and others
(see above examples)

Activity 3: Missing information: the Eurovision Song Contest

Type of activity
Information transfer

Main structures
Present Simple – question and answer forms (verb *to be*)
                  questions with *does*

Examples:
How old is Fleming Larsen?

Where does Marcel Meyer live?
Which country is 'Nana' singing for?
Is Paula Allen married or single?
etc.

Main functions
Asking for and giving personal information about other people
(see above examples)

Activity 4: Questionnaire: likes and dislikes

Type of activity
Questionnaire/discussion

Main structures
Like, love, don't like, etc. + noun
Like, etc. + gerund
So do I/Neither do I

Examples:

I like cats	Yes, so do I
I quite like writing letters	
I don't like washing my hair	No, neither do I
etc.	

Main functions
Expressing likes and dislikes (in varying degrees)
Agreeing or disagreeing with someone's likes and dislikes
(see above examples)

Activity 5: Who's who?

Type of activity
Information transfer

Main structures
Comparatives and superlatives of adjectives

Examples:
Peter is a year older than Sally.
The tallest person is a year younger than John.
etc.

Main functions
Asking for things to be repeated
Drawing conclusions
Asking for things to be confirmed

Examples:
Could you say that again?
So the girl on the left must be Sally.
Did you say that John is twenty-one next birthday?
etc.

Activity 6: One-sided dialogue: making suggestions

Type of activity
One-sided dialogue

Main functions
Asking for and making suggestions
Accepting or turning down a suggestion

Examples:
Shall we do something tomorrow?
How about . . .?
Why don't we . . .?
Let's . . .

No, I don't really like . . .
I'd rather not.
All right. Let's do that, then.

Activity 7: Following instructions (1)

Type of activity
Information transfer

Main structures
Imperatives
Prepositions of place

Examples:
Start in the black square.
Go to the square below the drawing of a house. In this square draw a large cross.
etc.

Main functions
Giving instructions
Asking for instructions to be repeated
Checking instructions

Examples:
I'm sorry, I didn't understand that. Could you say it again, please?
Did you say go left two squares?
etc.

Activity 8: Missing information: flats and houses

Type of activity
Information transfer

Main structures
Is there . . .?
Are there . . .?

Main functions
Asking for and giving information about flats and houses

Examples:
Where's the house?
Is the flat big?
Is the house modern?
How many rooms are there in the flat?
etc.

Activity 9: Following instructions (2)

See *Following instructions (1)*

Activity 10: This is my boyfriend/girlfriend

Type of activity
Simulation

Main structures
Question forms – various tenses
Questions beginning with a question word (*wh-* questions)

Examples:
Where did you meet him/her?
How long have you known him/her?
What's his/her job?
How old is he/she?
Do you plan to get married?
etc.

Main functions
Asking for and giving personal information
(see above examples)

Activity 11: Newspaper interview (1)

Type of activity
Role-play

Main structures
Future tenses – questions and statements

Examples:
When are you starting your march?
When do you hope to arrive in London?
Are you visiting many countries on the way?
What will you do about food?
etc.

Main functions
Asking and answering questions about future plans
(see above examples)

Activity 12: This is my brother

Type of activity
Simulation
(see *This is my boyfriend/girlfriend*)

Activity 13: Questionnaire: habits and daily routines

Type of activity
Questionnaire

Main structures
Adverbs of frequency – always, usually, often, etc.
'Do' questions

Examples:

Do you go out at weekends?	Yes, always
Do you remember your dreams?	No, not often
Do you find it easy to make friends?	Yes, usually
etc.	

Main functions
Asking and answering questions about habits and daily routines
(see above examples) ··

Activity 14: For sale

Type of activity
Simulation

Main functions
Describing things (a cassette recorder)
Asking and answering questions about something (a cassette recorder)

Examples:

What make is it?	It's . . .
How much do you want for it?	About . . .
Does it have a radio?	Yes, it does.
etc.	

Activity 15: Eye-witness

Type of activity
Role-play

Main functions
Describing someone (physical appearance)

Examples:
How old was he?
How tall was he?
Was he fat or thin?
What colour was his hair?
What was he wearing?
etc.

Activity 16: Complete the crossword

Type of activity
Information transfer

Main functions
Asking for and giving definitions of words

Examples:

What's 6 down?
What's 10 across?
etc.

You eat it. It's a fruit. It's yellow.
It's the opposite of 'hot'.

Activity 17: Carry on talking

Type of activity
Role-play

Main structures
Past tense – questions and answers

Examples:
Where did you go?
Were you alone?
What did you do?

Why didn't you phone me to let me know you weren't coming?
What was the party like?
Who was there?
etc.

Main functions
Talking about a pleasant event
Giving explanations
Talking about a party
(see above examples)

Activity 18: A family tree

Type of activity
Information transfer

Main structures
Present Simple – question word + verb *to be/have got*

Examples:
Who is Bill married to?
Is Paul a teacher?
How many children have Colin and Jennifer got?
Is Samantha nineteen?
etc.

Main functions
Asking for and giving personal information about people
Asking for confirmation that something is true
Saying that something is not true

Examples:
Who is Mary married to? She's married to Paul.
Is Samantha a hairdresser? Yes, that's right.
Is Pamela a shop assistant? No, she's not. She's a student.
etc.

Activity 19: Going on a weekend course

Type of activity
Simulation

Main structures
Would like . . .
Question word + verb *to be*
+ *will*

Examples:
I'd like some information about one of your weekend courses.
Where is it being held?
How much does it cost?
etc.

Main functions
Asking for and giving information about a course
(see above examples)

Activity 20: Complete the drawing (1)

Type of activity
Information transfer

Main structures
There is . . .
There are . . .

Where is . . .?
Where are . . .?

Prepositions of place

Examples:
There's a clock on the wall between the two cupboards.
There are three cups in the cupboard on the right.
Where's the jug?   It's . . .
Where are the glasses?   They're . . .
etc.

Main functions
Saying where things are in the kitchen
Asking where things are in the kitchen
Asking for something to be repeated
Asking for confirmation

Examples:
(see above examples)

Also:
I didn't understand that. Could you repeat it, please?
Do you mean here?
In which cupboard – the one on the right or the one on the left?
etc.

Activity 21: Complete the drawing (2)

As above, except that this activity is about saying where things are in the living-room.

Activity 22: Missing information: the life of Elvis Presley

Type of activity
Information transfer

Main structures
Past tense – questions with *did*
Past tense – *wh-* questions

Main functions
Asking for and giving information about a person's life
Narrating past events

Examples:
Where was Elvis born?
What happened to him in 1942?
What job did he get when he left school?
When did his mother die?
etc.

Activity 23: Looking at holiday photographs (1)

Type of activity
Simulation

Main structures
Questions and answers – Past tense

Main functions
Asking and answering questions about a holiday
Describing photographs

Examples:
Where did you go for your holiday?
How long did you stay in . . .?

Was it nice there?
Who did you go with?

What's this building here?
Who are these people?
Where was this photograph taken?
etc.

Activity 24: Newspaper interview (2)

See *Newspaper interview (1)*

Activity 25: Looking at holiday photographs (2)

See *Looking at holiday photographs (1)*

Activity 26: One-sided dialogue: shopping

Type of activity
One-sided dialogue

Main structures
I'd like + *some* + noun (countable, uncountable plural)
    + quantity + noun
Have you got . . .? + *any* + noun
How much + noun (uncountable)
How many + noun (plural, countable)

Examples:
I'd like two pounds of sugar, please.
Have you got any tins of tomato soup?
How much does it cost?
etc.

Main functions
Stating what you would like to buy
Asking how much of something someone wants
Inquiring about prices, brands, etc.
(see above examples)

Activity 27: Where's the station?

Type of activity
Information transfer

Main structures
Where is + building
Prepositions of place

Main functions
Asking about, and saying, where buildings are

Examples:
Where's the hospital?   It's in Green Road opposite the Chinese restaurant.
Where's the pub?   It's the first building on the left in London Road.
etc.

Activity 28: Questionnaire: opinions

Type of activity
Questionnaire/discussion activity

Main structures
Questions beginning with Do you think . . .?
Yes/No answers (Yes, I do/No, I don't/I'm not sure)
So do I/Neither do I

Main functions
Asking for and giving an opinion
Agreeing or disagreeing with an opinion
Stating uncertainty

Examples:

Do you think English is a difficult language to learn?	Yes, I do.	Yes, so do I. Do you? I don't.
Do you think politics is very interesting?	No, I don't.	No, neither do I. Don't you? I do.
Do you think men and women can ever be equal?	I'm not sure, really.	No, neither am I. Oh, I do. Oh, I don't.

etc.

Activity 29: Asking for information about a tour

Type of activity
Simulation

Main functions
Asking for and giving information about a tour

Examples:
I'd like some information about your coach tours.
Which tours have you got tomorrow, please?
When does the tour to Brighton leave London?
Where does the coach go from?
How much does it cost?
When does the coach get back to London?
Could I book two seats for the tour to Brighton, please.

Activity 30: Asking for information about summer jobs

As above, but this time asking for information about summer jobs.

Activity 31: One-sided dialogue: an invitation

Type of activity
One-sided dialogue

Main structures
Would you like to + verb phrase
What about + noun
When + *shall* + verb

Main functions

Asking how someone is (and answering)
Giving an invitation
Accepting an invitation
Turning down an invitation with a reason
Suggesting an alternative day
Arranging a time and place to meet
Confirming arrangements

Examples:

Hello, . . . How are you?   I'm all right, thanks. And you?

Would you like to go to the cinema with me next week?
Yes, I'd love to.
On Friday?   Oh, I can't, I'm afraid. I have to . . .

What about on Thursday? I'm free then.
Yes, Thursday would be fine.

What time?
Where shall we meet?

Right, I'll see you on Thursday, then.
Yes, I'll look forward to it.

Picture Credits